# Yolanda's
# Hand-Me-Down
# Recipes

Best Wishes
Yolanda Lodi

Also by Yolanda Lodi from Rock Village Publishing:
*Yolanda's Cranberry Country Recipes*

# Yolanda's
# Ḫand-Me-Down
# Recipes

by

Yolanda Lodi

Rock Village Publishing
Middleborough, Massachusetts

First Printing

# Dedication

To a great cook

my mother-in-law

Mary Lodi

# Introduction

**M**ost of the cooks who furnished recipes for *Yolanda's Hand-Me-Down Recipes* acknowledged the need to record favorite dishes for future generations to enjoy. In recent years my husband, Ed, continually reminded me that his mother is getting up there in age.

"She's got some great recipes, none of which are written down. Start recording them now. Don't wait till it's too late."

Last year around the holidays I took his advice. After jotting down Mary's instructions I proceeded to try out each recipe. In this collection of "hand-me-downs" I have included six of her most popular recipes. (Popular especially with Ed. He gave each the final seal of approval while enjoying every bite.)

Traditional Tortellini, the first hand-me-down in this collection, brought everyone together last New Year's Day. The time we spent reminiscing of years gone by made me appreciate traditions that are in danger of being forever lost. In the story following the recipe I've mentioned some of the highlights of that day.

One thing not mentioned is the day I invited my mother-in-law, Mary, to our house for Traditional Tortellini.

Shortly after arriving Mary asked: "When are we going to start making the tortellini?"

Looking at her with a smile, I said: "They're done. Ed and I made them yesterday. We had fun doing it. All that's left now is to cook them."

Throughout the meal Mary kept saying: "Couldn't be better," to both the tortellini and the Stuffed Shells—another favorite recipe of Mary's included in this collection.

Some of the recipes in this book which appear simple were in fact a challenge to perfect.

I wrestled quite a bit with the Welsh Rabbit. Luckily, the third time proved a charm. Be sure to slowly whisk the paste into the hot milk. Otherwise the paste forms lumps and the rabbit never thickens. Remember the hare and the tortoise? Be slow like the tortoise and be sure to use a double boiler.

Do you still have your pressure cooker? Use it to cook the beets for Ensalada de Remolacha. Since I don't have one I wrote the recipe according to how I prepared it.

Every single recipe, with the exception of the three contained in the section, "Thanksgiving in the Barn," has been tried by me and approved either by the person who furnished the recipe or by family and friends. Maybe some Thanksgiving I'll be able to take Sue Lyons up on her invitation to join her family and friends in their unique holiday tradition.

Every cook, it seems, has his or her own method for cooking salt cod. After making Bolo de Bacalhau I brought a portion for Alice Costa to sample.

"Perfect. Though mine is saltier," she said.

Alice soaks the salt cod for at least 24 hours, changing the water 3 or 4 times. Then she cooks the cod well, but only once. I cook it twice. Since everyone today is concerned about salt intake, I've included her recipe the way I make it.

You may have heard of Plymouth Rock eggs. They're laid by an American breed of hens known for their super large eggs. In My Dad's Sponge Cake, I learned recently, "Dad" always used these eggs when making his sponge cake. His neighbor raised Plymouth Rock hens for their eggs and meat. I haven't come across any, but if you do, give them a try. According to Evelyn, his daughter, that's the secret to a great sponge cake.

Speaking of secrets, I'm convinced that coffee is the secret ingredient in Hermit Cookies. Everyone who sampled these cookies could not guess that they contained coffee. Not even my mother-in-law, Mary. She kept saying to her son, "Your father loved hermits. It's been years since I've made them. I don't think I remember the recipe."

It's been more than ten years since Mary last baked hermit cookies for her husband. Hardly a day goes by, I'm sure, that she fails to think about all the wonderful recipes she cooked over the years for her family. Today, at age 89, Mary still cooks up a storm. She's a great cook and I feel privileged to be her daughter-in-law. ❧

# Contents

## Poultry ⬅ Seafood 🐟 and More

### Poultry

### Seafood

### More

# Soups 🍲 Salads 🥢 and Sauce

## Soups

## Salads

## Sauce

# 🥧 Desserts 🥞

## Cakes

## Cookies

# Poultry

## Seafood

### and More

## TRADITIONAL TORTELLINI

### Chicken / Vegetable Broth

1 split chicken breast (about ½ pound)
2 carrots
1 onion
1 ripe tomato
1 stalk celery

Place chicken breast and peeled vegetables (whole) in a large pot. Cover with *cold water*. Bring to a boil.

Reduce heat to simmer. Cover and cook for about 1½ hours until chicken is tender.

Remove cooked chicken from broth. Remove meat from bones and cut into small pieces. Discard skin. Set aside for the *Ripieno.*

Remove cooked vegetables. Refrigerate. (No longer needed for this recipe.) Strain broth. Set aside ¼ cup broth for the *Ripieno.*

Refrigerate the remaining broth in the same large pot, to be used later to cook the tortellini.

## Ripieno
## (Stuffing)

1 cup Parmesan cheese, freshly grated
¼ cup *Broth*
¼ tsp. ground black pepper
⅛ tsp. salt

Prepare food processor for chopping.

Place cut-up chicken in work bowl. Pulse until shredded.

Transfer shredded chicken to a medium-size bowl. Add above ingredients. Combine with a spoon. *Ripieno* should be moist, not wet.

Cover with plastic wrap. Refrigerate.

## Sfogia

4 extra-large eggs
3½ cups all-purpose flour
2 Tbsp. olive oil
2 Tbsp. water

Prepare food processor with dough blade.

Place all ingredients in work bowl. Pulse until the dough comes together.

Using your hands knead dough into a ball. Place *Sfogia* ball on a lightly floured tablecloth (clean, of course). Cover with a bowl for 30 minutes.

*Continued...*

## Stuffing the Sfogia:

Assemble pasta machine. Lightly sprinkle flour on tablecloth.

Cut a slice of *Sfogia*. Cover remaining *Sfogia* with bowl until ready to be used.

With disk of pasta machine at maximum setting feed the *Sfogia* through rollers. Repeat this process several times, reducing the setting each time, ending with the tightest setting.

Place flattened *Sfogia* on lightly floured tablecloth. Cut into 2-inch squares. Form the tortellini by placing a small amount of *Ripieno* in the center of the square. Fold edges over to form a triangle. Press the two edges tightly to seal, twisting each end. Holding the tortellini in your left hand bend the left twisted corner back, then bend the right twisted corner back to meet its mate. Pinch to seal, forming a ring.

Allow tortellini to dry on the tablecloth for 4 to 6 hours before refrigerating.

Refrigerate in a paper bag.

*Cooking the Tortellini:*
1 can (48 oz.) chicken broth

Remove large pot containing *Broth* from refrigerator. Skim off the fat. Add can of chicken broth to pot. Bring to a boil.

Add *Tortellini* to boiling broth. Cook until *al denté*, about 4 to 5 minutes.

Remove from stove.

Serve with freshly grated Parmesan cheese.

Makes 8 to 10 servings.

**Note:** If serving tortellini the same day, no need to dry. Proceed to *Cooking the Tortellini.*


*O*n New Year's Eve I learned how to make Traditional Tortellini from the experts: my mother-in-law, Mary, and her sister Annie. It had been thirty years since either of them had tackled tortellini. With no written recipe to refer to, the ladies put on their cooking caps. After some discussion and sharing of fond memories, Mary and Annie agreed on the recipe. Ready with pen and paper, I recorded the details, including a tidbit or two.

While I prepared the food processor Mary said: "Years ago I used a large wooden board to mix and knead the sfogia."

Continued...

# Poultry  Seafood  and More

"Yes. Dad would place the board on the table," Ed added, remembering his early childhood when his mother would spend hours in the kitchen cooking and baking. In those days every meal was a feast.

"I piled a mound of flour in the center of the board, formed a well in the middle, and added eggs, oil, and water," Mary continued.

"Extra-large eggs?" I interrupted, with an eye on her egg carton.

"Yes. I always use extra-large eggs," Mary replied. "I covered the well with flour and kneaded the dough till it formed a smooth ball. Sometimes I added a little more flour. Sometimes water. I never measured. I always knew when it was ready to rest for thirty minutes."

"Remember the long rolling pin, Mary?" Annie said.

"Long rolling pin?" I asked.

"Yes. About this long." Mary held her hands about three feet apart.

Annie chuckled. "Yes. I inherited half of one. Years ago someone cut Ma's long rolling pin in half. I don't know who has the other half."

Sometime in the 1960's Mary's husband surprised her with a pasta machine — IMPERIA — Made in Italy. The pasta machine made Mary's own long rolling pin obsolete.

ແ

*Wanting to surprise my husband with his mother's Traditional Tortellini, I shopped for a pasta machine and found the exact same machine. Forty years later and stores still import IMPERIA from Italy!*

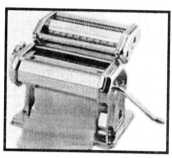

*As I paid for my purchase the sales clerk commented: "That's a great pasta machine. Years ago when my children were little I bought an electric one. Noisy! And you had to precisely measure the dough ingredients, otherwise the pasta would stick to the rollers. And what a lot of work to clean. This one's great. Plus children can get involved in rolling the dough. That's the difference in families today. Years ago families spent more time together—cooking, eating, talking."*

*After leaving the store I thought about the fun I'd had learning how to make tortellini with my husband and his aunt and mother. It turned out to be a two day social event: the first day making the*

*Continued...*

tortellini, the second day cooking and eating them.

When I arrived home that evening I couldn't contain myself. "Honey, you won't believe this. I just bought the same pasta machine as your mother's."

And thanks to Mary and Annie the tradition continues. They took the time and had the patience to teach me how to make this special tortellini. (As a novice, it took me many tries to get the "twist" and "pinch" just right so the stuffing wouldn't fall out.)

And Ed—looking forward to future feasts—couldn't be happier.

## CRANBERRY CHICKEN CASSEROLE

1 whole chicken (2 ½ - 3 lbs.), cut-up
¼ cup olive oil
- salt to taste
- pepper to taste

Preheat oven to 325 degrees.

Wash and dry chicken pieces. In a large skillet heat the oil over medium heat. Add chicken pieces. Brown chicken in oil 15 to 20 minutes. Season with salt and pepper.

Drain the chicken well. Place the chicken pieces in a 2-quart oven-proof baking dish.

### *Sauce*

1 Tbsp. olive oil
½ cup onion, chopped
½ cup celery, chopped
1 cup whole cranberry sauce
½ cup catsup
2 Tbsp. lemon juice
1 Tbsp. brown sugar
1 Tbsp. Worcestershire Sauce
1 Tbsp. prepared mustard
1 Tbsp. vinegar

In a large skillet heat the oil over medium heat. Add onion and celery. Sauté until tender, but not

*Continued...*

browned (about 5 minutes). Stir in the remaining
*Sauce* ingredients.

Pour *Sauce* over chicken. Bake **uncovered** at 325
degrees for 1 hour and 15 minutes, basting
occasionally during baking.

Makes 4 servings.

*A*nytime I hear the words "cranberry recipe"
my ears perk up.

*Recently when I overheard my good friend Anne
explaining to a group of women how she makes
Cranberry Chicken Casserole, I eagerly asked:
"Where did you get the recipe?"*

*Anne replied: "From my son, Ray." Without
pausing to take a breath she preceded to tell me
that his first big job as a chef was at The Quechee
Inn in Vermont. That's where she and her friend
Betty first tasted Cranberry Chicken Casserole.*

*Shortly after Betty returned home she contacted
Anne for Ray's recipe. Well, the rest is history. For
the last twenty years Anne has shared her son's
recipe with all of her friends.*

*Today, Ray owns The Oar House Restaurant,
located on the waterfront in historical downtown
Portsmouth, New Hampshire. Upon returning
home my husband and I raved to friends about*

the gourmet lunch we had there. That was a few years ago, before the writing of any cookbooks. We hope to return there some day soon.

This recipe is a "hand-me-down" in reverse: son to mother. Do you agree?

# WRAPPED TURKEY BREAST

3 lbs. boneless turkey breast

## Sauce

2 Tbsp. butter or margarine, melted
2 Tbsp. grated Parmesan or Romano cheese
1 tsp. cornstarch
¼ tsp. dill weed
¼ tsp. dried basil leaves
⅛ tsp. ground black pepper

Preheat oven to 350 degrees.

Combine *Sauce* ingredients in a small bowl. Set aside.

Place turkey on a sheet of heavy foil, large enough to double fold on top and sides. Spoon *Sauce* over turkey.

Bring up edges of foil over turkey and double fold. Complete *packet* by folding ends twice to seal.

Place *packet* in a roasting pan.

Bake at 350 degrees for two hours and twenty minutes.

Unwrap *packet* carefully. Transfer cooked turkey to serving platter, then slice. Pour juices into a gravy boat to serve with turkey.

Makes 6 servings.

*A* couple of years ago when my husband and I vacationed in California, the most enjoyable part of our stay was the time we spent in Davis with Aunt Annie and Uncle Harry. Their traditional New England salt box, with its colonial decor inside and manicured gardens outside, recreates the atmosphere of a bygone era—peaceful and relaxing.

One morning Annie announced that the evening's meal would be roasted turkey.

"Can I help?" I asked, thinking of all the work cooking a turkey would necessitate.

"Sure," Annie replied. "It won't take long. When we return from Sacramento this afternoon we'll get the turkey in the oven."

"What time will we eat?" I silently wondered.

ଓଃ

That afternoon Annie and I prepared Wrapped Turkey Breast in a snap.

While the turkey cooked we sipped iced tea and reminisced of our happy times in California. It was a tranquil scene, with Morris, Annie's beloved cat, curled up in one of the patio chairs; Lester, the neighbors' 'fraidy cat, crouched behind the gazebo at the far end of the garden; the neighborhood pet rabbits hopping across the lawn—probably in search of Harry's prized tomato plants—and birds flitting to and from the feeder.

*Continued...*

*WRAPPED TURKEY BREAST...Continued*

*Later, after Harry said grace, I thought: "What a feast! And so simple to prepare." I made up my mind that from now on this would be the turkey I would serve for Thanksgiving. Thanks to Annie, my husband and I enjoy this hand-me-down recipe year 'round.*

# THANKSGIVING

## IN THE BARN

# MOM LYONS'S TURKEY STUFFING

## Broth

> 5 stalks celery, whole
> 3 medium onions, whole
> ¼ tsp. salt
> • gizzards, heart, liver, neck from 1 turkey

Place the above ingredients in a medium saucepan. Cover with water. Simmer on the stove for 1 hour.

Cool.

> 5 slices bread, toasted
> 1 cup *Broth*
> ½ cup (1 stick) butter
> 1 pkg. (14 or 16 oz.) Herb Seasoned Stuffing
> • Bell's Seasoning to taste

Drain and reserve *Broth* from cooked turkey parts.

Remove meat from neck. Grind together with heart and liver. Place in *large bowl*. (Discard gizzards.)

Place toasted bread in another bowl. Pour cold water to cover bread. Squeeze the water out of the bread. Add squeezed bread to *large bowl*.

In a small pan heat 1 cup *Broth*. Add butter. Stir until butter melts.

Remove from stove. Cool slightly.

Add broth / butter liquid to *large bowl*. Stir in stuffing mix. If needed, add *Broth*, one teaspoon at a time, until well blended and moist. Season to taste.

> ***Note:*** *Broth* is also used in Aunt Beansie's Gravy recipe.

## *"WILD TURKEY" TURKEY*

> 1 cup Wild Turkey liqueur
> 2 Tbsp. soy sauce
> 2 Tbsp. lemon juice

Mix above ingredients in a small bowl.

Use this sauce to baste turkey during the last 2 hours of cooking.

# AUNT BEANSIE'S GRAVY

*(Made from the water used
to cook fresh vegetables)*

Reserve the following water from cooked vegetables:

1 cup carrot water
1 cup potato water
½ cup onion water

1 cup *Broth* (reserved from Mom Lyons's Turkey Stuffing recipe)
1 cup water
5 Tbsp. all-purpose flour
1 tsp. Gravy Master
• salt to taste
• pepper to taste

Remove cooked turkey from roasting pan. Pour water from cooked vegetables into roasting pan containing drippings from roasted turkey. Add *Broth* and stir.

In a small bowl combine water and flour until mixture resembles pancake mix. Stir in Gravy Master.

Add this mixture to liquid in roasting pan. Stir. Add salt and pepper to taste.

Strain gravy into a saucepan.

Heat before serving.

Makes 8 to 12 servings.

*T*he above three recipes are very special to Sue Lyons. Until now they had never been written down.

About 35 years ago, because their dining room table was no longer large enough to accommodate their family and friends, Sue's Aunt Beansie and Uncle Bob moved their traditional Thanksgiving feast outside—to the barn behind the house. Although Uncle Bob had retired from building boats in the barn, he still maintained the heating system, oil and an old pot belly stove. To make room for his growing family Bob built long tables out of planks and provided folding chairs in

*Uncle Bob*

*Continued...*

*different styles. Everyone had a seat and a place at the table.*

*Uncle Bob did all the preparations, except pluck the turkeys and make the gravy. Thanksgiving morning at the crack of dawn, to make sure there was plenty of turkey to feed thirty to forty people, he placed at least three birds in the ovens. He peeled the vegetables the night before. Aunt Beansie's specialty was making the gravy.*

*Everyone arrived carrying an accompaniment, such as scalloped oysters, cranberry orange mold, and littlenecks (dug by Sue's father) on the half shell. Desserts consisted of assorted fruit pies and Indian pudding, along with Aunt Beansie's Pineapple Cream Squares.* (For the recipe turn to the dessert section.)

*Earlier in the day Sue and her cousins dressed up the barn using old sleds, duck decoys, and other items that Aunt Beansie had found at yard sales. Some of the items still had the prices on them, such as the little plastic pumpkins with the tag, "10¢," attached.*

*"Each year my Aunt and I would scour the countryside for dried cornstalks with which to decorate as well," said Sue. "That is, until we grew older and wiser and realized we could use the same stalks year after year!*

*"After dinner we showed home movies of grand-parents who had passed on, and of ourselves*

*with our Easter bonnets, or on Christmas eves and mornings skating at Capron Park in Attleboro, Massachusetts, and sliding down the hills. After almost four decades we continue to look forward to Thanksgiving in the barn.*

*"What are your plans for Thanksgiving this year?" Sue asked. "There's always room for more, like the year we had a basket of beagle puppies beside the wood stove."*

*What a wonderful tradition to look forward to each year.*

## MRS. BRITTO'S JAG

½ cup large lima beans
2 Tbsp. olive oil
1 medium onion, chopped
½ cup fresh mushrooms, sliced
1 can (6 oz.) tuna, drained
2 cups boiling water
1 packet Sazón Goya Con Azafran
1¼ cups rice

### *The Day Before Cooking:*

*Soak the lima beans overnight in 2 cups of cold water.*

### Cooking Day:

Gently drain and rinse the beans. Place the beans in a large pan with 2 cups of cold water.

Heat to boiling. Reduce heat to medium and cook until skins fall off the bean (about 20 minutes). Drain water and set aside.

In a 3-quart pan heat the olive oil over medium heat. Add onions and mushrooms. Sauté until soft, but not browned.

Stir in tuna. Add cooked beans and stir.

Reduce heat to medium-low. Pour boiling water into saucepan. Stir in one packet Sazón Goya. Add rice. Check to be sure there's enough rice by placing a soup spoon in the center of the pan. Spoon stands up for a second by itself when there's enough rice. Adjust accordingly.

Reduce heat to low. Cover and simmer for 20 to 25 minutes.

Makes 4 to 6 servings.

*L*ena Britto was born in 1921 in Rochester, Massachusetts. Her parents immigrated from Cape Verde. Family values of love, hard work, and good traditional Cape Verdean food, such as jagacida, have carried her through her joyful journey in life.

*During one of our sessions with Mrs. Britto (my husband is helping her write her memoirs), she surprised us with her special jag made with canned tuna from* Cabo Verde *(TUNNY FISH Packed by* Sociedade Ultramarina de Conservas, LDA).*

*"This is the best jag we've ever had," Ed and I told her.*

*"Could you give me the recipe?" I asked.*

*That week I attempted to make Mrs. Britto's Jag. Delicious, but the rice wasn't as fluffy as hers. What could her secret be?*

Continued ...

*Jag...Continued*

*"I always use Uncle Ben's rice," she told me over the phone. "Are we getting together Sunday? Have the lima beans ready and I'll cook the rice when I get there."*

*Sunday after Mrs. Britto arrived I started making her jag. She added the boiling water and rice while I watched. Placing a soup spoon in the center of the pan, she released it for a second saying, "Enough rice. The spoon stands up."*

*We covered the pan, leaving it to simmer for 20 minutes. In the meantime I took note of the approximate quantity of boiling water and rice used by Lena, who, like many good cooks, does not use exact measurements.*

*Twenty minutes later when I removed the cover from the pan I exclaimed, "The rice exploded. It's so fluffy and light!"*

*The three of us sat down to another memorable meal of Mrs. Britto's Jag while she continued to tell us more about her childhood experiences and accomplishments. She conveys them with such humor that laughter always fills the room.* Yankee Mericana: My Cape Verdean Odyssey *by Lena Britto is scheduled for publication in early 2002. For a taste of Cape Verde try Mrs. Britto's Jag along with her book of memoirs.*

*\* Best tuna to use for this recipe. Packed in an 11 oz. can. Use a little bit more than half of the can. As Mrs. Britto said to me, "I use the remaining tuna in a sandwich for lunch."*

# FILLET OF FLOUNDER WITH CHOPPED QUAHOGS AND SHRIMP SAUCE

24 fillets of flounder (sole or similar)
18 medium quahogs (2½-inch x 3¼-inch hard shell clams)
1½ cups plain bread crumbs
3 to 4 Tbsp. sour cream
24 round toothpicks

Steam quahogs to open. **Do not cook.** Shuck and chop coarsely into one-half inch chunks (1½ cups needed). Reserve *shell liquor.*

Combine chopped quahogs and bread crumbs. Mix thoroughly. Add sour cream to make a firm dough. Add reserved *shell liquor,* up to ¼ cup, to just loosen mixture.

Lay out fillets, smooth side up. Place two heaping teaspoons of quahog mixture on double tab end. Roll fillet on slight diagonal so single tab crosses center line. This prevents roll up from breaking in two. Pin roll up together with *round* toothpick (flats are too weak) through single tab.

Pack roll ups in one layer in a 12- x 9- x 4-inch baking dish, tight with tab side up. A typical arrangement provides three rows of eight roll ups.

Preheat oven to 350 degrees.

*Continued ...*

## Sauce

3 cans (10 ¾ oz. each) cream of
   shrimp soup
1 can (6 oz.) small or medium shrimp,
   *drained*
½ cup dry white wine
¼ cup fresh parsley, chopped
• Lea & Perrins Worcestershire Sauce
   to taste

Mix cream of shrimp soup, drained shrimp, wine, and parsley. Slowly add Lea & Perrins until mixture has the right zip. (Start with 1 Tbsp.)

Pour *Sauce* over roll ups. Bake **uncovered** at 350 degrees for about 20 minutes, or until sauce bubbles all around.

Makes 24 roll ups.

# Poultry 🐟 Seafood 🐚 and More

*Mr. Stewart A. Washburn graciously shared his favorite seafood recipe with me, which he found filed within a cookbook while cleaning out his Aunt Annie's back porch.*

*"What's this?" he said to himself.*

*"Quahogs. I like quahogs." So he kept the recipe, he tells me.*

*"It belonged to my grandmother, Mrs. Parker, who lived in New Bedford, Massachusetts, and enjoyed cooking, especially when she had kitchen help. She used a simple white sauce. To streamline the recipe I developed my own shrimp sauce."*

*He included with his recipe this tidbit of advice: "Experiment with Lea & Perrins. Add slowly until the mix has the right zip. The oyster bars which Savarin used to run from Boston to Baltimore in the main railroad stations added Worcestershire to stews and pan roasts. Always a secret amount and always to good effect."*

*I hope you find the right zip when whipping up this newly favorite recipe of mine.*

# SCALLOPED OYSTERS

1 pint fresh oysters
2 cylinders Ritz Crackers, crushed into crumbs
1 cup half-and-half
1 Tbsp. butter or margarine

Preheat oven to 350 degrees.

Butter an 8- x 2-inch round glass oven-proof baking dish.

Sprinkle *one-third* cracker crumbs over bottom of the dish. Top with *half* of the oysters. Add another *one-third* of cracker crumbs, followed by remaining oysters. Finish with remaining cracker crumbs.

Pour half-and-half over entire casserole. Dot with butter.

Bake at 350 degrees for 35 to 40 minutes, until bubbly and lightly browned.

Makes 6 servings.

# Poultry 🍗 Seafood 🐟 and More

*Fifty years ago—as now— commercial fishermen on Cape Cod worked long and hazardous hours earning a living from the sea. Even so, they always managed to share some of their bountiful catch with relatives and friends. One such man was Carlton.*

*Because my mother-in-law, Mary, was friends with Frances, Carlton's wife, she received fresh oysters, along with Frances's Scalloped Oysters recipe—which Mary still uses today.*

*These days Mary purchases fresh oysters at her local fish market. How do they compare to Carlton's oysters of years ago?*

*"Still fresh," Mary says. "But without the work of having to open them. No matter how careful my husband was, he often sliced his hands on the sharp edges of the shells."*

*Ask my own husband, Ed, who grew up in Wareham surrounded by beaches, and he'll tell you how plentiful oysters were thirty or forty years ago and how he used to gather them by the bushel. They're not nearly so plentiful now. And a bad back prevents Ed from gathering his own.*

*So imagine his delight the other evening when I surprised him with Scalloped Oysters. "I'm glad you got the recipe from my mother," he said. "I never thought I'd eat this again!"*

*Once you try Scalloped Oysters, you'll want to delight others with it, too.*

## *Bolo de Bacalhau*

½ lb. boneless dried salt cod fillet
6 large potatoes, cut lengthwise in
   julienne strips
4 beaten eggs
¼ cup olive oil
4 medium onions, thinly sliced lengthwise
2 garlic cloves, chopped
2 Tbsp. parsley, chopped
• ground black pepper to taste
• bread crumbs to cover cake

*The Day Before Cooking:*

*Place the salt cod in a glass bowl and cover it with cold water. Cover the bowl tightly with plastic wrap. Soak the cod in the refrigerator overnight.*

Cooking Day:

Rinse the salt cod. Place the cod in a pan. Pour enough cold water to cover the cod.

Cover and cook over medium heat, bringing water to a boil.

Drain water.

Repeat the preceding three steps (rinsing, cooking, draining).

Cod is cooked when you can flake it with a fork.

Drain water and set aside to cool.

Lightly fry the potato strips. Do not let them brown. Drain on paper towels.

Finely flake the cooked cod fillet. Remove skin, if any. Set aside.

In a large pan heat the olive oil over medium heat. Add onions, garlic, parsley, and pepper. Sauté until soft, but not browned.

Using a wooden spoon stir in flaked cod until combined. Slowly add the fried potatoes, stirring constantly to prevent mixture from sticking to pan.

Reduce heat to low. Stir in beaten eggs. Continue to stir (about 10 minutes), until mixture starts to form a ball.

*Continued ...*

*Bolo de
Bacalhau*

*BOLO DE BACALHAU...Continued*

Pack mixture into bundt pan. With a knife, loosen mixture from edges, then invert cake onto serving platter. Cover cake with bread crumbs.

## *Alice's Suggestions*

❖ Use an old linen napkin to flake cod. Place cod in the middle of the napkin. Tie ends together with a string. Using both hands rub the cod and napkin together until cod is finely flaked.

❖ Lightly sprinkle chopped parsley on top of cake.

❖ Fill the hole in the center of the cake with large black olives.

❖ Surround cake with salad or rice.

Makes 8 to 10 servings.

*Maria do Ceu grew up in Vila de Rei, a small village in Portugal. Occasionally she received invitations to family celebrations in Lisbon. Intrigued by the big city, she looked forward to these special times.*

*During one of her visits to Lisbon, Maria do Ceu was treated to a memorable casserole dish. Before leaving for home she obtained the recipe from her hostess.*

Maria do Ceu began making this codfish recipe at home, serving it with large pitted black olives, a village tradition. Throughout the years she made changes to the recipe to suit her family's taste.

A couple of years ago her daughter, Alice Costa, asked for the recipe. She was throwing a party and wanted a special fish dish.

"You had french fries when you lived in the village?" Alice asked, puzzled—remembering her own childhood before the family emigrated to Fall River, Massachusetts, when she was about twelve.

"No," her mother explained. "In those days I used whatever potatoes I had on hand. Eventually I discovered that french fries give the casserole a better taste."

The night of the party Bolo de Bacalhau made its debut. Because she enjoys being creative, Alice transformed her mother's casserole dish into a cake by using a bundt pan and adding bread crumbs to the top and sides. Even Al, Alice's husband, who is not fond of cod, couldn't resist a slice of bolo (cake). Now he enjoys cod whenever Alice makes her Bolo de Bacalhau.

At your next party, you may want to surprise your guests with this very special cake.

# NELLIE'S WELSH RABBIT

  2 cups whole milk
  ½ lb. mild cheddar cheese, cut into small
    pieces
  1 egg, whisked
  1 Tbsp. dry mustard

### *Paste*

  2 Tbsp. all-purpose flour
  2 Tbsp. *cold* milk
  1/16 tsp. ground cayenne pepper
  • salt to taste

Stir *Paste* ingredients in a small bowl until well blended.

In another bowl mix cheese and egg.

### ☙

In a double boiler over high heat bring milk to a boil. Reduce heat to medium.

When milk stops boiling **slowly** whisk in *Paste*. **Slowly** add dry mustard. Continue to whisk in one direction until mixture thickens.

**Slowly** add cheese and egg mixture. Stir constantly with a spoon until cheese melts, and Rabbit is smooth, velvety, and piping hot.

Serve hot over dry toast or crackers.

Makes 4 to 6 servings.

*N*ellie developed her special Welsh Rabbit when she belonged to the Ladies Temperance Union, an organization that totally abstained from alcoholic beverages. Instead of the traditional beer, she substituted milk and omitted the butter. Whenever she had guests for lunch on Fridays, especially during Lent (Nellie was Catholic), the entrée most likely would be Welsh Rabbit, a dish that originated in Wales and later became a British and American favorite.

Today Nellie's granddaughter, Anne Wolf, continues the tradition in Rochester, Massachusetts. Whenever her brother, Bud, visits all he has to say is: " I could go for some Welsh Rabbit." Without hesitation Anne cooks-up their grandmother's favorite Friday lunch, serving Nellie's Welsh Rabbit over Uneeda Biscuits, the same crackers Nellie invariably served more than forty years ago. Although Nellie has been gone many years, Anne has fond memories of her each time she makes this recipe.

Incidentally, the name for this popular dish has an interesting history. In the eighteenth century the English tended to look down upon the Welsh, whom they considered poor and uncouth. So poor were the Welsh that many could not afford meat; as a consequence they developed wholesome and flavorful dishes made from cheaper ingredients, such as bread and cheese.

Continued ...

*WELSH RABBIT...Continued*

As a cruel joke, the supercilious English referred to the most popular Welsh dish as "Welsh Rabbit." In time, forgetting the origin of the name—and noting the absence of rabbit—people assumed that rabbit must be a corruption of rare-bit. Thus you'll often see recipes for "Welsh Rare-bit."

(For the benefit of any scholars who may be reading this, my husband, who has researched the matter, informs me that according to the Oxford English Dictionary, the term Welsh Rabbit first appeared in 1725. But it wasn't until sixty years later, in 1785, that Welsh Rare-bit made its debut.)

## A REAL TABOULI RECIPE

½ cup fine bulgur wheat
2 large bunches fresh parsley
½ bunch scallions, finely chopped
1 small cucumber, diced
3 or 4 medium-size tomatoes, diced
Seasonings to taste:
- salt
- ground black pepper
- ground allspice
- dried mint, crushed (a pinch)
¾ cup lemon juice
¼ cup olive oil
1 or 2 lemons

Soak bulgur wheat in *cold* water for 20 minutes, or until soft and swollen.

While the bulgur wheat soaks, remove parsley stems by hand. Discard stems.

Snip the parsley leaves with kitchen scissors or chop with a knife. (Not too fine.) Place parsley in a colander. Rinse with cold water. Set aside.

Drain bulgur wheat. Squeeze dry with your hands and place in a large bowl. Then squeeze parsley dry. Add to bulgur wheat and toss until combined. Fold in scallions, cucumber, and tomatoes.

Sprinkle seasonings, one at a time, over top of

*Continued ...*

mixture, stirring each time.

Add lemon juice and olive oil. Stir until all ingredients are combined.

Cover and refrigerate 2 to 3 hours for full flavor.

When ready to serve, toss the tabouli until all ingredients are combined. Transfer to serving dish and squeeze fresh lemon juice over entire top.

## *Barbara's Suggestions*

❖ Use curly parsley. Easier to snip or chop.

❖ Use locally grown mint.

❖ Best time for making tabouli is in the summer, when tomatoes are fresh. To add flavor to winter tomatoes, add ¼ cup lemon juice to diced tomatoes.

❖ Surround serving dish with Romaine lettuce leaves *before* squeezing fresh lemon juice over tabouli.

❖ Best served between lettuce or pita bread. Place a spoonful of tabouli on a leaf of lettuce or a piece of bread. Fold over to form a bite-size sandwich.

Makes 6 to 8 servings.

# Poultry 🐔 Seafood 🐟 and More

*T*o quote Barbara: "Store-bought tabouli is loaded with bulgur wheat and doesn't contain nearly enough parsley. Real tabouli consists of lots of fresh parsley with lemon juice."

*A Real Tabouli Recipe was handed down from Barbara's grandmother, who was born in Lebanon and grew up in Virginia before marrying and settling in Fall River, Massachusetts, in the 1930's. When her son married, his Irish wife, Madeline — discovering how much her husband loved tabouli—quickly learned how to make it.*

*By the time Barbara was born, Madeline had a reputation for making better tabouli than her mother-in-law. Perhaps it was her adding a small diced cucumber for bulk that made the difference.*

*Today Barbara carries on the tradition of making tabouli, especially for large family get-togethers. Among those who eagerly look forward to her tabouli is, of course, her Italian husband.*

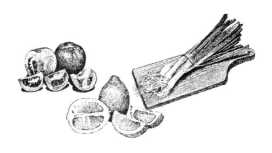

# MARY'S RISOTTO

2 Tbsp. butter
1 Tbsp. olive oil
1 medium onion, diced
1 cup long grain rice or Arborio rice
2 cans (14.5 oz. each) chicken broth
1 cup cooked peas
• grated Parmesan cheese to taste

In a frying pan heat the butter and olive oil over medium heat. Add onions. Sauté until translucent, but not browned (about 5 minutes).

Add rice. Stir well until rice is coated.

**Slowly** stir in chicken broth. Continue stirring until rice is cooked and mixture thickens. Fold in cooked peas. Stir until rice absorbs all the liquid.

Serve with grated Parmesan cheese on the side. Sprinkle on top of risotto to own taste.

Makes 4 servings.

*This recipe originated in the late Eighteen Hundreds. My mother-in-law, Mary, remembers her mother always making risotto as a main entrée.*

*"I just love it," Mary says. "I eat it by itself."*

*Over the years Mary made changes in her mother's recipe to expedite cooking, such as using canned chicken broth instead of home-made. Also, she'll cook-up frozen peas instead of using fresh ones.*

*Every time Mary invites Ed and me for dinner, if there's rice to accompany chicken, it's risotto. Mary will say to me: "I know you don't like peas, so I didn't add too many. Hope you don't mind."*

*Well, I now eat peas. Mary's Risotto made a pea lover of me.*

## BABA GHANNOOJ

1 lb. eggplant, whole with skin
1½ garlic cloves, peeled and minced
¼ tsp. salt
¼ cup tahini sesame purée
• lemon juice squeezed from one lemon

Roast the eggplant over high heat. Keep turning the eggplant over the open flame until tender.

When slightly cool, scoop eggplant from skin into a bowl, removing some of the seeds. Don't worry if pieces of skin accompany the scooped eggplant. This will give the Baba Ghannooj a smoke flavor.

In a separate bowl combine the minced garlic and salt. Stir in tahini and lemon juice. Add the roasted eggplant. Mix well until all ingredients are combined.

Serve with pieces of pita bread. Dip right in. No utensils needed.

Makes 2 servings.

*Note*: For best flavor roast the eggplant on an outside grill. To oven cook, place whole eggplant in center of baking dish. Bake at 450 degrees until tender (about 25 minutes), turning frequently during cooking.

*Tony at his Lebanese restaurant, River Cafe*

"*Our pleasure is to serve you—for it is with our hearts that we offer you our tables.*"

*In a totally unexpected place—Hallowell, Maine—my husband and I experienced what for us has been the ultimate in dining.*

*With a population of only 2500, Hallowell— which neighbors the capitol, Augusta— is the smallest city in Maine. Upon checking in at our home for the next three days, Maple Hill Farm B & B, my husband and I asked innkeepers, Scott and Vince, for their recommendations of restaurants in the area. The one that struck an immediate cord: River Cafe, a Lebanese restaurant.*

*Continued ...*

"*I feel adventuresome today. Let's experience a Lebanese feast,*" *I said.*

*My husband, knowing how fussy I can be, said:* "*You surprise me.*"

ଔ

*Looking over the menu I spotted Vegetarian Maza:* "*A tantalizing combination of Mid-East dishes, selected to complement each other and satisfy your tastes. Experience it!*"

"*Honey, let's get this for two.*" *(Also available for four and six.)*

"*Are you sure?*" *Ed asked.*

"*Yes. I'm even going to order Lebanese wine. I'm going all the way.*"

*Of the appetizers, I pounced on the Baba Ghannooj, a dip consisting of eggplant (one of my favorites) and tahini.*

"*Honey, you pick the other two.*"

*Knowing that I'm not fond of stuffed rolled grape leaves, Ed selected other items.*

"*No stuffed rolled grape leaves?*" *I asked in front of the waitress.* "*You're always eating them from a can for lunch.*"

*Our appetizers arrived with a basket of fresh pita bread, along with one stuffed rolled grape leaf.*

"*You must try this,*" *our waitress said, eager to see our reaction.* "*Mama makes them herself.*"

*"This is delicious!" we both exclaimed simultaneously.*

*"Nothing like the ones in a can," I said. "Next time we'll order these."*

*As part of the feast two vegetarian entrées followed the appetizers. At the end of our meal I said to the waitress: "This has been a great dining experience. I'd love to include Baba Ghannooj in the cookbook I'm currently working on."*

*Antoine (Tony) Younes, proprietor of River Cafe, immigrated with his family fourteen years ago to escape the war in Lebanon. He and his family took the plunge and opened River Cafe. Tony's mother and brother are still preparing their family recipes.*

*"One thing we know is how to cook. This recipe is very old. Baba Ghannooj developed in the Middle East hundreds and hundreds of years ago. We use no measurements. Every mother teaches her daughter to cook."*

*Tony graciously handed me this recipe, saying: "People need to try our food."*

*As Ed and I were leaving we caught a glimpse of Mama. Her smile lit up the room. We left Hallowell wanting to return soon, not only to try other dishes on the menu, but to spend more time conversing with Tony, who made us feel like one of the family.*

# STUFFED SHELLS

  1  medium butternut squash, cut in half
     lengthwise and seeds removed
  1  package (12 oz.) jumbo pasta shells,
     cooked according to package instructions
     (*al denté*)
  ¼  tsp. ground nutmeg
  2  cups Parmesan cheese, freshly grated,
     plus extra if needed
1½  cups pasta sauce

Coat a glass oven-proof baking dish with olive oil.
Place squash cut-side down.

Bake at 350 degrees for 55 minutes or until squash is
tender.

### *Squash Filling*

When slightly cool, scoop squash from skin into a
large bowl. With electric mixer at low speed, blend
until smooth. Add nutmeg and 1 cup cheese.
Combine with a spoon. Taste. If needed, add more
cheese.

Grease the bottom of a 13- x 9-inch glass oven-proof
baking dish.

Spread a thin layer of pasta sauce on the bottom.

Using a large spoon stuff each cooked shell with
*Squash Filling* and place in baking dish. Pour
remaining sauce over the stuffed shells. Sprinkle
remaining cheese over top. (Add more cheese if you
prefer "loads of cheese.")

Bake at 350 degrees for 20 to 25 minutes.

Makes 6 to 8 servings.

*A lice, who seldom cooked but who enjoyed
home-made food, gave her sister-in-law
Mary this recipe for stuffed shells many years
ago. Alice said that her brother Jake created the
recipe. Jake loved to cook and grew his own
vegetables. What better way to use fresh
butternut squash?*

*Alice died several years ago and Jake recently
passed away. Although they're both gone, their
stuffed shell recipe lives on. Because I knew both
of them, this recipe is a special "hand-me-down."*

# Soups

## Salads

### and Sauce

# DORTHY'S CREAM OF TOMATO SOUP

2 large onions, diced
1 large green pepper, diced
1 large sweet red pepper, diced
1 cup water
½ cup (1 stick) butter
2 Tbsp. sugar
1 tsp. salt
1 tsp. ground black pepper

Place above ingredients in a large soup pot. Stir occasionally over medium heat until mixture begins to boil. Reduce heat to low. Cover and simmer until vegetables are tender.

Add the following in the order listed:

4 cans (14.5 oz. each) stewed tomatoes with onions, celery, and green peppers
¼ tsp. baking soda (Be sure to add baking soda **before** adding milk to prevent curdling.)
4 cans (14.5 oz. each) whole milk (To measure, use empty stewed tomato cans.)
1 lb. American cheese, cut into small to medium pieces
• salt to taste
• ground black pepper to taste

Increase heat to medium high. Heat soup until hot, stirring frequently. **Do not boil.**

Makes 12 to 14 servings.

*A*fter watching her mother and her mother's cousin in Nova Scotia preparing something similar, Dorthy improvised and came up with this recipe.

"They made the soup with fresh tomatoes. To remove the skins they put the tomatoes in a pot of boiling water, allowing them to sit for a bit, then draining the water. The skins literally fell off. They added milk and that was it. I can remember Mum saying: 'Always add a bit of baking soda to make the tomatoes alkali instead of acid, so it won't curdle when you add the milk.' I use canned stewed tomatoes (no salt added) when fresh tomatoes are not in season."

Dorthy continues her mother's tradition of making Cream of Tomato Soup when tomatoes are available from local farmers. Since the tomato season is so short and soup is appreciated more during the cold winter months, Dorthy chose her version of her mother's recipe to be the hand-me-down for future generations to enjoy.

"Besides it's the recipe I use the most frequently."

# DORTHY'S CORN CHOWDER

4 medium potatoes, peeled and finely diced
1 large onion, diced
1 large green pepper, diced
1 medium sweet red pepper, diced
1 cup water
½ cup (1stick) butter
1 tsp. salt
1 tsp. ground black pepper

Place above ingredients in a large soup pot. Stir occasionally over high heat until mixture begins to boil and butter melts. Reduce heat to low. Cover and simmer until vegetables are tender.

Add the following ingredients in the order listed:

2 tsp. sugar (Omit if cream-style corn contains added sugar.)
4 cans (14.75 oz. each) cream-style corn
4 cans (14.75 oz. each) whole milk (To measure, use empty corn cans.)
- salt to taste
- ground black pepper to taste

Increase heat to medium high. Heat soup until hot, stirring frequently. **Do not boil.**

Makes 12 to 14 servings.

# Soups 🍲 Salads 🥣 and Sauce

*D*orthy developed this recipe twenty years ago after having corn chowder for the first time at a restaurant in Dedham, Massachusetts. Every Wednesday she and her girlfriend looked forward to having lunch together at a different restaurant, with the opportunity to try something different. Admiring the appearance and taste of the chowder, Dorthy returned home that day to try her hand at making her own version.

Because she prefers not to thicken soups with flour, she decided to dice the potatoes into very small pieces. Remembering the green pepper in the restaurant chowder, she added some along with sweet red pepper.

"Red pepper gives the chowder more flavor and color," Dorthy says. "Also, I chose the creamed corn to help make the soup thick and to eliminate the use of cream. I use whole milk instead."

Although the restaurant did not give the recipe to Dorthy in writing, they introduced her to the taste of corn chowder. Her determination to recreate the taste resulted in Dorthy's Corn Chowder, a unique hand-me-down recipe, don't you think?

## MARINATED BROCCOLI

3 large bunches fresh broccoli crowns, raw
1 cup cider vinegar
1 cup olive oil
1 Tbsp. dill weed
1 Tbsp. Ac'cent® Flavor Enhancer
1 Tbsp. salt
1 Tbsp. sugar
1 tsp. ground black pepper
1 tsp. garlic powder

Rinse broccoli. Remove stems. Place broccoli crowns in a large rectangular container that has a sealed cover.

In a large (two-cup) measuring cup combine the remaining ingredients. Pour the mixture over the raw broccoli. Seal with cover and refrigerate.

Marinate in the refrigerator for 8 to 24 hours. Shake container occasionally.

When ready to serve, remove broccoli with slotted spoon.

Makes 8 to 10 servings.

# Soups  Salads and Sauce

*L*ast Christmas I served Marinated Broccoli. Everyone loved it, including my aunt, who's not crazy for broccoli.

*This recipe arrived by mail a few weeks before the holidays, compliments of a mutual broccoli lover whom I met at a craft fair in Hanover, Massachusetts. Hearing that I was compiling a book of hand-me-down recipes, Kathy told me about this one.*

*Kathy does not know the origin of Marinated Broccoli. An Army wife gave her the recipe twenty years ago when their husbands were Airborne / Rangers with the 2 / 325 at Fort Bragg, North Carolina. To quote Kathy: "I've served Marinated Broccoli since then with rave reviews. It's a great appetizer at cookouts while waiting for food to grill. And one way to get kids to eat broccoli. I know you'll enjoy it, too."*

*I'll say!*

# ENSALADA DE REMOLACHA

2 bunches beets, leaves removed (or six
beets, the size of lemons)
- salt (a pinch)

### Dressing

1 medium onion, finely chopped
1 medium tomato, diced
½ cup cilantro leaves, finely chopped
¼ cup lemon juice (squeezed from
one lemon)
- salt to taste

Place beets in a large pan and cover with cold water.
Add a pinch of salt, cover and bring to a boil.

Reduce heat to medium. Cook covered until tender,
about 35 to 40 minutes.

Drain water and rinse immediately with *cold* water.
Peel and dice beets into a large bowl.

In a separate bowl combine *Dressing* ingredients. Pour
over diced beets and toss well.

Cover and refrigerate 2 to 3 hours. Serve chilled.

When ready to serve, toss the Ensalada until all
ingredients are combined. Transfer to serving dish.

## Maria's Suggestions

❖ Go light on the salt.

❖ Best if refrigerated overnight

❖ Serve on a bed of lettuce in individual salad bowls. Add a slice of avocado.

Makes 6 to 8 servings.

*aria Torres has fond memories from childhood of her mother's colorful beet salad. Never one to serve a plain green salad, Gilma routinely included her Ensalada de Remolacha with family meals. That was more than forty years ago.*

*Today, sixteen years after immigrating to the United States from Colombia, Gilma continues to serve her Ensalada, especially when she invites her daughter and family for Sunday dinner. Gilma's traditional Sunday feast includes: soup, entrée accompanied with plantain or rice, and salad— always Ensalada de Remolacha.*

*Does Maria make Ensalada de Remolacha for her husband and daughter?*

*"Once in a while. But it's never like my mother's. Hers is the best."*

# Soups 🫕 Salads 🍃 and Sauce

## ANTIPASTO FROM THE WEST COAST

1 jar (6 oz.) marinated artichoke hearts,
   **including** liquid
1 can (14 or 15 oz.) wax yellow beans,
   drained
1 bottle or jar (10 oz.) cocktail onions,
   drained
1 can (6 oz.) pitted black olives, drained
1 can (8 oz.) button mushrooms, drained
1 can (14 or 15 oz.) kidney beans, drained
1 can (14 or 15 oz.) garbanzo beans, drained
⅓ cup balsamic vinegar
¼ cup chopped parsley
2 tsp. Italian seasoning, plus extra if needed
1 tsp. dried basil leaves

Place all of the above ingredients in a large glass salad bowl. Stir lightly. Cover bowl tightly with plastic wrap.

Refrigerate overnight.

Makes 8 servings.

### Irene's Suggestions

❖ On hot summer evenings serve this antipasto as a dinner. Serve with bread, wine, and fruit.

❖ For those who do not care for garbanzo beans, use a can of green beans instead.

# Soups 🍲 Salads 🥗 and Sauce

*T*his antipasto recipe has been handed down several times to people in different states. The recipe originated in California with Mary Lou, who handed it to her dear and close friend, Anne Miller, who also lives in California and spends some time in Arizona. Anne then gave the recipe to her sister, Irene Martin, who lives in Arizona with her husband, Donald. She has been making this antipasto since 1966, especially on hot summer evenings when one does not want a hot meal.

*"It is easy to make,"* Aunt Irene tells me during her recent vacation to Massachusetts. That, and Mary Lou, is why I include this recipe.

*When my husband and I were vacationing in California a couple of years ago, Mary Lou and her husband, dear friends of Aunt Annie and Uncle Harry, invited the four of us to dinner at their home, a beautiful ranch outside of Sacramento, California. Ed and I will always remember the gourmet feast we had, accompanied with exquisite wine. The whole evening is one we will treasure, surrounded by family and friends, and the natural beauty of their home. Sometimes I wonder if it wasn't a dream. The evening was perfect, just like Antipasto From the West Coast.*

# KAREN'S CRANBERRY MOLDED SALAD

1 pkg. (6 oz.) cranberry-flavored gelatin
2 cups sugar
2 cups boiling water
1 pound cranberries
1 apple, peeled and cored
1 cup crushed pineapple with juice
1 cup seedless red grapes, cut in half
¾ cup miniature marshmallows
½ cup finely chopped walnuts

In a large bowl mix the gelatin and sugar. Pour boiling water, stirring until gelatin and sugar dissolve. Set aside to cool, but not set.

While waiting, grind together the cranberries and apple. Add the remaining ingredients: pineapple, grapes, marshmallows, walnuts. Fold all ingredients into cooled gelatin mixture. Pour into a mold or large bowl to set.

Refrigerate until firm.

Makes 10 or more servings.

### Karen's Suggestions

❖ For a firmer set, add one packet Knox unflavored gelatin.

❖ Make the day before serving. The longer the salad sets, the tastier it gets.

# Soups  Salads and Sauce

*B*arbara Winters from Jackson, Michigan, sent me this recipe. I met Barbara and her husband at an Elderhostel program that my husband and I attended on Campobello Island, New Brunswick, last fall. After seeing my recently published cookbook, **Yolanda's Cranberry Country Recipes**, *she started to tell me about this delicious recipe that all her family and friends enjoy. She got the recipe from her daughter-in-law, Karen, who had gotten it from a friend many years ago.*

*By the time this cookbook is published Mr. and Mrs. Winters will have celebrated their 50th Wedding Anniversary. Their anniversary is in August; their children gave them an Elderhostel to Hawaii for September.*

*Cranberries do get around. It's exciting to know that out in Michigan cranberry recipes are being handed down to family and friends. Hope you give this one a try and add it to your collection of special cranberry treats.*

# WHOLE BERRY SAUCE

3  cups whole cranberries, fresh or frozen
1  cup sugar
½  cup water

Combine all ingredients in a 2-quart saucepan. Cover pan tightly.

On high heat bring to a *full* boil. When you hear the *full* boil, remove lid immediately and reduce heat to medium. Do *not* stir!

Cook for 25 to 30 minutes, occasionally shaking saucepan back and forth. Do *not* stir!

Cool.

Cover saucepan and refrigerate overnight.

Makes 2 cups.

# Soups 🍲 Salads 🥗 and Sauce

*W*hen he was growing up my husband, Ed, always looked forward to his mother's *Whole Berry Sauce* at Thanksgiving and Christmas and on other special occasions. Although Mary no longer cooks her holiday feasts, she carries on part of her tradition by bringing her special cranberry sauce to our holiday gatherings.

*Last Thanksgiving I asked Mary for her recipe. As she recited the instructions from memory I smiled from ear to ear. Every time she emphasized: "Do not stir," I couldn't help thinking of Sophie J's Cranberry Chutney, a recipe from my* Cranberry Country Recipes *that requires a full thirty minutes of stirring.*

*Whole Berry Sauce is a great recipe with which to impress your guests. It's a no-fail sauce so long as you remember: Do* not *stir!*

# Desserts

# Mary's Butternut Squash Pie

2 cups butternut squash, cooked
*(see following recipe for Cooked Butternut Squash)*

4 large eggs
1 can (12 oz.) evaporated milk
1 cup *less* 1 Tbsp. sugar
1 tsp. cornstarch
1 tsp. ground cinnamon
1 tsp. ground nutmeg
¼ tsp. ground ginger
• pastry for a single-crust pie

Preheat oven to 350 degrees.

Pastry-line a 9-inch glass pie plate, folding excess pastry under and back to form a one-inch rim, then flute.

Place all ingredients (except crust, of course) in a large bowl. With electric mixer at low speed, blend until smooth.

Pour filling into pastry shell.

Bake at 350 degrees for about one hour, or until knife inserted in center comes out clean.

Cool on a wire rack.

Makes 8 servings.

## COOKED BUTTERNUT SQUASH

### *for Mary's Butternut Squash Pie*

1 medium butternut squash, cut in half lengthwise and seeds removed

Coat a glass oven-proof baking dish with olive oil. Place squash cut-side down.

Bake at 350 degrees for 55 minutes or until squash is tender.

Cool slightly.

Scoop squash from skin into a two-cup measuring cup.

*D*uring butternut squash season Mary religiously bakes her son's favorite pie. Well, one of his two favorite pies. Ed's other favorite is Mary's Mock Cherry Pie (included in my Cranberry Country Recipes cookbook). I know Ed's favorite foods because I'm his wife. Since I take advantage of all opportunities to score with my man, I asked Mary for her recipe.

As she gave me the recipe she recounted its history: "Alma, the same dear friend who gave me the cranberry pie recipe gave me this one. She worked for rich people and often baked pies for them. That was in 1930, when we were both nineteen years old."

*Continued ...*

*Mary grew silent, then continued: "Alma died at the age of fifty. Although she's been gone forty years I still think of her."*

*Over the years Mary modified Alma's recipe to suit her own taste, never, however, recording the exact measurements. Thanks to their friendship and Mary's love for baking (from memory—she seldom writes down her recipes) I now have the recipes for Ed's two favorite pies.*

*Perhaps you have someone special you'd like to bake a pie for?*

# AUNT BEANSIE'S PINEAPPLE CREAM SQUARES

## Crust

1 cup (2 sticks) butter, softened
2 cups all-purpose flour
4 tsp. granulated sugar

Preheat oven to 350 degrees.

Combine all *Crust* ingredients in a bowl. Stir with a spoon. Then blend well by hand to form a ball.

Place ball in the center of an **ungreased** 13- x 9-inch pan. Using your palm and fingers press dough evenly and firmly onto the bottom of the pan.

Bake at 350 degrees for 15 to 20 minutes, or until *Crust* is light brown.

Cool on wire rack.

*Continued ...*

## Desserts

### Filling

- ½ cup (1 stick) butter, softened
- 1½ cups confectioners' sugar
- 2 Tbsp. pineapple juice (only enough to make mixture easy to spread)

In a small bowl, with mixer at low speed, cream butter and sugar. Add pineapple juice, a little at a time, until mixture is light and fluffy. Frost **cooled** *Crust* with this mixture.

### Topping

- 1 pint heavy cream
- 1 can (20 oz.) *crushed* pineapple, *drained*

Beat cream until stiff. Fold in pineapple. Spread evenly over *Filling*.

Makes 12 servings.

**Note**: Cool Whip can be used instead of heavy cream.

*T*his recipe is very popular with Sue Lyons's family at Thanksgiving. (See Thanksgiving in the Barn.) *In my opinion, Pineapple Cream Squares are perfect any day of the year.*

*Having made this recipe just once, I fell in love with it. And I'm not overly fond of whipped cream. (I'll order an ice cream sundae without it.) When I offered my friends a taste all I heard was: "These are delicious! Could I have another?"*

*Not only are these squares light and tasty, they're also easy to make. I'm looking forward to the next time I whip up a batch.*

# CAVACAS
# by KELLY

9 jumbo eggs
2 cups all-purpose flour
1 cup Mazola® Corn Oil

Preheat oven to 350 degrees. Spray twenty-four 2½-inch-muffin-cup pan with non-stick cooking spray.

Place all ingredients in a large bowl. Mix at medium speed for about 25 minutes.

Spoon or pour evenly into muffin cups.

Bake at 350 degrees for 35 minutes or until puffed and well browned.

Remove from oven. Tilt muffin pan until cavacas fall onto wire rack. Cool **completely**.

Glaze cavacas with the following sugar glaze recipe:

## Sugar Glaze
3 cups confectioners' sugar
3 Tbsp. *cold* water

Combine all *Sugar Glaze* ingredients in a bowl. Spread glaze on top of each cavaca. Allow cavacas to dry for two to three hours before storing in a non-airtight container.

## Kelly's Suggestion

❖ Measure 1 cup confectioners' sugar in a large
(one-cup) measuring cup. Add 1 tablespoon of
*cold* water. Mix well with a spoon. Glaze to taste.
Repeat until all cavacas are glazed.

Makes 24 cavacas.

"*My* grandmother Maria was born in Quintela
de Azurara-Mangualde," Kelly Costa told
me. "As a young girl she was taught a number of
skills, cooking being one of them. She learned to
make many delicious treats, but most were
made only on holidays or for special functions.
My Mom, the eldest of her four children, picked
up her skills. She learned to knit, sew, cook, and
bake. One of the treats she makes most often is
the cavacas."*

*Cavacas. I had forgotten about this special
childhood treat that my father on occasion
would bring home from the Portuguese bakery.
As a child I loved the sweetness of the sugar
glaze and the puffiness of the cookie-like pastry.
These memories resurfaced when Kelly
mentioned her Cavacas recipe. I knew I wanted
to make these to share with family and friends
who have never had them. They're like Kelly —
unique and fun. I must add: Kelly turns 21
this year.*

# DOUG'S NUTTY CRANBERRY BREAD

             2 cups all-purpose flour
             1 cup sugar
          1½ tsp. baking powder
             ½ tsp. baking soda
             ½ tsp. salt
             1 egg, well beaten
             • juice and rind from one orange
             2 Tbsp. butter
             • boiling water
             1 cup chopped walnuts
             1 cup sliced raw cranberries
             1 ripe banana, mashed

Preheat oven to 350 degrees.

Grease and flour a 9- x 5- x 3-inch loaf pan.

Sift flour. Add sugar, baking powder, soda, and salt.
Sift again into a large bowl.

Stir in beaten egg.

Put orange juice, rind, and butter in a measuring cup.
Add boiling water to fill to the ¾ mark. Stir into flour
mixture.

Fold in walnuts, cranberries, and mashed banana.

Pour batter into loaf pan.

Bake at 350 degrees for 1 hour or until toothpick
inserted into center comes out clean.

Cool 15 minutes, then remove from pan.

Makes 1 loaf.

*In 1962 Doug, one of the recipients of the Key Award given to outstanding 4-H Club members for their excellence and outstanding accomplishments, represented Massachusetts at the "Big E" in Springfield, Massachusetts. Expecting to do either horse or dog demonstrations (his forte) during the long weekend, he was caught completely off guard when he found himself in the Massachusetts State Building baking cranberry bread, the state's feature item that year, for the public to sample.*

*Over the years Doug made several changes to the original recipe. The change most enjoyed by his family and friends is the added ripe mashed banana, which makes for a very moist bread. The combination of cranberry, banana, and orange ensures a different fruit taste at every bite.*

*"Don't let a lack of a fresh orange stop you from making this bread. Just pour 1/4 cup orange juice into a measuring cup. Add the 2 tablespoons of butter and then proceed to pour boiling water to fill to the 3/4 mark. This recipe is so easy I make several breads at one time—and none ever make it to the freezer. My family and friends make sure of that."*

# Aunt Mary's Rice Pudding

    3 cups cooked rice
    1 can (12 oz.) evaporated milk
    3 large eggs, beaten with a fork
    1 cup sugar
    2 Tbsp. (¼ stick) butter
    • salt (a pinch)
    • ground cinnamon to taste

In a medium-size pan combine the cooked rice and milk. Stir over medium heat until mixture begins to boil. Reduce heat to low.

Gradually add beaten eggs, stirring constantly until combined.

Increase heat to medium. Add sugar, butter, and pinch of salt. Continue stirring until pudding begins to boil. Immediately remove from heat; otherwise the eruptions, like molten lava, may burn you.

Spoon into dessert dishes. Sprinkle with cinnamon.

Makes 8 servings.

# Desserts

*When I was twenty and dating Bob I met his Aunt Mary, a widow of many years who loved to cook. One of her Portuguese specialties was rice pudding.*

*Shortly after Bob and I married, Aunt Mary—knowing how much her nephew loved her rice pudding—surprised me with the recipe. For years I made the pudding according to her oral instructions.*

*Aunt Mary died in 1992, the same year that my marriage to Bob ended. The other day I came across a tattered scrap of paper with the following:*

Put in pan bowl of water. Boil with 1 c. of rice. When rice is cooked, 1 can of PET milk. Stirring. Beat 3 eggs. Add to pan. Also 1 c. of sugar. ¼ bar of butter. Pinch of salt.

*After several tries and many dishes of rice pudding (my husband, Ed, enjoying every mouthful), I now have Aunt Mary's rice pudding exactly as I remember it.*

# GRAND PÉRE'S

## A Fruit Dumpling Dessert

1 can (21 oz.) raspberry or blueberry
   pie filling
½ can (10.5 oz.) water (To measure, use
   empty pie filling can.)
½ cup sugar
• salt (a pinch)

Combine all ingredients in a 3-quart pan. On medium heat bring to a continuous *slow* boil. While waiting, prepare *Flour Mixture*.

## Flour Mixture

1 egg
½ cup whole milk
1 cup all-purpose flour
½ tsp. baking powder

Beat the egg and milk until foamy. Slowly add flour and baking powder. Batter forms "a ribbon" when spoon moves back and forth across top of batter. If needed, add pinches of flour until "ribbon" effect is achieved.

Using a large serving spoon, drop (evenly spaced) eight individual balls of batter on top of the *slow* boiling fruit. Cover. Cook till puffy, about ten

minutes. Turn the dumplings over. Cover. Cook again till puffy, about another ten minutes.

Spoon into dessert bowls. Serve warm with whipped cream.

Makes 8 servings.

*A*s a child Flora loved to watch her mother make dumplings. "My mother was a great cook. She never measured. Having ten kids she was always throwing something different together."

When Flora married she continued her mother's custom of making fruit dumplings, especially raspberry, Flora's favorite. Ask one of her sons, Bob: "My mother's Grand Pére's — delicious— hot and doughy— surrounded with fruit—sweet with loads of whipped cream. My favorite when I was a child, and still is. Debbie and I always look forward to my mother's Grand Pére's."

"Bob" is Robert Duff, the artist of the painting on the cover of this cookbook. He and his wife Debbie own the Duff Gallery in New Bedford, Massachusetts. As busy as they are they never pass up an opportunity to sit down and enjoy dumplings made from a recipe that goes back more than a century.

# TOMATO SOUP CAKE

½ cup shortening
1 cup sugar
1 egg
1 can (10¾ oz.) tomato soup
2 cups all-purpose flour
2 tsp. baking powder
1 tsp. ground cinnamon
1 tsp. ground nutmeg
⅛ tsp. ground cloves

Preheat oven to 350 degrees.

Generously grease and flour an 8-inch round pan.

In a large bowl, with mixer at low speed, cream shortening and sugar. Beat egg into creamed mixture until smooth and fluffy. Add tomato soup. Mix at low speed until well blended. Mixture will look curdled.

Sift together the remaining ingredients (flour, baking powder, cinnamon, nutmeg, cloves). Add to creamed mixture, a little at a time, beating after each addition.

Spoon batter into pan. Bake at 350 degrees for 45 to 50 minutes or until toothpick inserted into center comes out clean.

Cool cake **before** removing from pan. Frost cake with the following frosting recipe.

Friday, August 11, 1950

223rd Day — 142 days to follow

CLEAR
CLOUDY
RAIN
SNOW

Sift dry ingredients
+ add to creamed mixture

## Tomato Soup Cake

½ cup shortening
1 cup sugar
2 cups flour
2 teaspoons baking powder
1 tsp. cinnamon
1 " nutmeg
dash cloves
1 egg — 1 cn. tomato soup

Cream shortening and
sugar. Add egg
beat into creamed
mixture, Then add
tomato soup mix
well. Add flour a
litte at a time and beat
Bake in 350° oven
1 hr.

Continued ...

*TOMATO SOUP CAKE...Continued*

## Cream Cheese Frosting

4 oz. cream cheese, softened
2 cups confectioners' sugar
1 tsp. vanilla extract

Place all frosting ingredients in a large bowl. Beat until smooth and fluffy.

Makes 1 cake.

*argaret Andrews passed away in 1982 at the age of 77. While cleaning her home Mitzi Booker, her granddaughter, found the recipe for Tomato Soup Cake written on a piece of paper torn from an appointment book.*

*It was during World War II when Margaret first started baking this cake. Ingredients such as butter were scarce, so Margaret used what was readily available. Her Tomato Soup Cake became so popular that whenever a special occasion arrived family members would ask Margaret to bake her unique cake.*

*Margaret never recorded the recipe for her cream cheese frosting. After talking with Margaret's daughter, Mary Booker, I jotted down the following: "Cream cheese at room temperature; add confectioners' sugar and vanilla extract. That's all my mother did."*

Mary added: "Sometimes my mother added nuts or raisins. She also sprinkled chopped walnuts on top of the frosted cake."

As a child Mitzi remembers her grandmother's Tomato Soup Cake and how at first she made a face. "Can you believe it? A cake made with tomato soup!"

Today this is Mitzi's favorite. She continues to keep the August 11, 1950, note in the same old cookbook that belonged to her grandmother. The paper is yellow and brittle and falling apart at the creases, but to Mitzi it's a treasure, one that she refers to every time she makes her grandmother's sensational Tomato Soup Cake.

Why she recorded the recipe on August 11, 1950, no one knows. We're so glad she did.

# AUNT LO'S COFFEE CAKE

1 cup (2 sticks) butter or margarine
1 cup granulated sugar
1 cup sour cream
2 eggs
1 tsp. vanilla extract
2 cups all-purpose flour
1 tsp. baking soda
⅓ tsp. salt


### Topping

1 cup chopped walnuts
⅓ cup brown sugar
¼ cup granulated sugar

Preheat oven to 325 degrees.

Grease and flour a 13- x 9-inch pan.

In a large bowl cream butter and sugar. Add sour cream and eggs, one at a time, beating well after each addition. Add vanilla.

Sift together the remaining ingredients (flour, baking soda, salt). Add **slowly** to batter, mixing well after each addition. Set aside.

Place all *Topping* ingredients in a small bowl. Mix well.

Spread half of the batter into the baking pan.

Sprinkle half of the *Topping* over the batter. Using a spatula spread the remaining batter. Finish by sprinkling the remaining *Topping*.

Bake at 325 degrees for 35 minutes or until toothpick inserted into center comes out clean.

Makes 1 coffee cake.

*T*his is a prize winning recipe. Back in the 1940's Donald Martin's Aunt (pronounced "Ant" in the West) Lo developed this recipe and won a monetary prize for it. No one in the family recollects the details and Aunt Lo is no longer around to ask.

*Donald's wife, Irene, is one of the few people that has recorded hand-me-down recipes in cookbook form for herself and her daughters-in-law. And no, I'm not one of them, but I can call her Aunt Irene. I'm married to her nephew.*

*Back to the recipe. Aunt Irene remembers Aunt Lo saying, "Use real sour cream. Sprinkle the topping in the middle of the batter and on top of the batter. Don't mix the topping with the batter. Sprinkle."*

*East meets West thanks to Aunt Irene recording Aunt Lo's Coffee Cake recipe.*

# MY DAD'S SPONGE CAKE

    3 large eggs, separated
    ²/₃ cup cold water
    1¼ cups granulated sugar
    1½ cups all-purpose flour
    1 tsp. baking powder
    1 tsp. vanilla extract
    1 tsp. cider vinegar
    ¼ tsp. almond extract
    • confectioners' sugar to sift over top

Preheat oven to 350 degrees.

Grease a 13- x 9-inch pan.

In a bowl beat egg **yolks** well. Add cold water. Beat until foamy. Add sugar and beat for 6 minutes.

Sift flour and baking powder together 3 times. Add to **yolk** mixture. Mix until combined.

In another bowl beat egg whites till stiff. Gently fold them into **yolk** mixture. Stir in vanilla, vinegar, and almond.

Pour batter into pan. Bake at 350 degrees for 30 minutes.

Remove pan from oven and turn upside down on wire rack to cool. When cooled, transfer cake to serving plate and sift confectioners' sugar over top. Serve with strawberries and whipped cream.

Makes 1 cake.

# 🥧 Desserts 🍰

*For the last 35 years Ruth Brown, our typographer for Rock Village Publishing, has faithfully attended Evelyn's Christmas Cookie Exchange. Knowing that Evelyn is not only a great cook but has won awards for some of her specialty dishes, Ruth asked her for a recipe to include in this cookbook.*

*When Ruth handed the recipe to me I exclaimed: "Evelyn Pursley! Mrs. Pursley taught at Fairhaven High School when I was a student there. I graduated in 1972."*

*Evelyn included the following note with the recipe:*

*"This cake recipe is over seventy years old. I have always called it 'My Dad's Sponge Cake' because he made it only when my mother was ill, or on the occasion when my brother was born. He never baked anything else, and he never cooked at any other time.*

*"It was delicious with strawberries and whipped cream. It's the best sponge cake I have ever had."*

# *AUNT GRACE'S FRUIT CAKE*

- ⅓ cup shortening
- 1 cup brown sugar
- 1 cup candied cherries, whole or chopped
- ½ cup candied pineapple, chopped
- ½ cup mixed candied fruit with citron
- ½ cup dates, chopped
- ½ cup figs, chopped
- ½ cup golden raisins
- ½ cup chopped walnuts
- 1 tsp. ground cinnamon
- ½ tsp. salt
- ⅓ tsp. ground cloves
- ¼ tsp. ground nutmeg
- 1 cup water
- ½ cup brandy

Combine above ingredients in a large pan. On high heat stir to boiling. Boil and stir for 3 minutes. Remove from heat.

Let stand to **cool** about 30 minutes.

Preheat oven to 350 degrees.

Coat a 9- x 5- x 3-inch loaf pan with non-stick cooking spray.

Add the following ingredients to your **cooled** fruit mixture in the order listed, **stirring after each addition**:

> 1 tsp. baking soda
> 2 cups all-purpose flour
>    (Add one cup at a time.)
> ½ tsp. baking powder
> ¼ cup water

Pour batter into loaf pan.

Bake at 350 degrees for about one hour.

Makes 1 cake.

## *Priscilla's Suggestion*

❖ After spreading batter evenly in loaf pan, decorate the top of the fruit cake with walnuts and whole candied cherries.

*Continued ...*

# Desserts

"*G*race Weber Hoxie grew up in West Roxbury, Massachusetts, and her brother, Leslie Weber, married my Mom's sister, Wanda Dobachewski," Priscilla A. Porter informed me. "Grace Hoxie—or 'Aunt Grace' to us—was a wonderful cook. The fruit cake recipe was passed down in her family for several generations.

"My Mom, Helen Dobachewski Porter, also grew up in West Roxbury at the Brook Farm Home for Children. She went to live there when she was 4 years old, along with her two sisters and one of her brothers. Her other two brothers were sent to live and work on a farm in Warren, Massachusetts. The Home was owned and operated at that time by the Lutheran Church. A Lutheran Minister and his wife lived there with the children, along with their own children."

Priscilla sent Aunt Grace's Fruit Cake recipe to me along with the story. When their Mom passed away she and her sister put together a cookbook for their family.

At Christmas their Mom would spend weeks baking many goodies for family and friends, especially Aunt Grace's Fruit Cake.

**CR**

"My Mom was a wonderful cook and baker," Priscilla said, after I handed her a piece of the fruit cake I had baked earlier.

*I could smell the fruit and spices permeating through the plastic wrap. "This fruit cake is moist, loaded with fruit, and rich with spices," I said. "I found it easy to make. Nothing like any fruit cake I've had in the past."*

*As I was leaving, Priscilla mentioned her family's favorite, Apple Sauce Cake, and how her mother got the recipe. "It's easy to make," Priscilla added.*

*As you may guess, the next recipe is Apple Sauce Cake, along with the continued story.*

# APPLE SAUCE CAKE

1 cup **cold** apple sauce
1 tsp. baking soda
½ cup shortening
1 cup sugar
2 cups all-purpose flour
1 cup raisins
1 tsp. ground cinnamon
½ tsp. ground cloves

Preheat oven to 350 degrees.

Grease and flour a 9- x 5- x 3-inch loaf pan.

Combine apple sauce and baking soda in a small bowl. Set aside.

In a large bowl, using a spoon, cream shortening, adding sugar gradually. Add apple sauce mixture and stir.

Add the remaining ingredients (flour, raisins, cinnamon, cloves). Stir until combined.

Pour batter into loaf pan.

Bake at 350 degrees for 50 to 55 minutes.

Makes 1 cake.

(This story is continued from the previous recipe, Aunt Grace's Fruit Cake.)

*A*pple Sauce Cake was Priscilla's Mom's favorite cake as a child when she was growing up in Roxbury, Massachusetts, at the Brook Farm Home for Children. When she left the Home, knowing the only way she would have Apple Sauce Cake again would be to make it herself, Helen asked the Minister's wife for the recipe.

*Over the years Helen enjoyed this special treat from her childhood along with sharing special stories with her children. Even though Helen is gone now, the memories shared by her daughters still live on with their Mom's Apple Sauce Cake recipe.*

*Whenever Priscilla makes this cake she likes to frost the top and sides of it. I asked her: "What kind of frosting?"*

*She replied: "Oh, just regular frosting, nothing fancy, but be sure to add almond flavoring. It tastes great. My family loves it!"*

# LAZY DAY CAKE

1¼ cups boiling water
1 cup Quick oats
½ cup (1 stick) butter or margarine
1 cup granulated sugar
1 cup firmly packed brown sugar
1 tsp. vanilla extract
2 eggs, beaten with a fork
1½ cups all-purpose flour
1 tsp. baking soda
¾ tsp. ground cinnamon
½ tsp. salt
¼ tsp. ground nutmeg

In a large bowl pour boiling water over the oats and butter. Cover. Let stand 20 minutes.

Preheat oven to 350 degrees.

Generously grease a 9-inch square pan.

Add sugars to oat mixture. Stir. Add vanilla and beaten eggs. Mix well with a spoon.

Sift together the remaining ingredients (flour, soda, cinnamon, salt, nutmeg). Add to mixture. Stir until combined.

Pour batter into pan. Bake at 350 degrees for 50 to 55 minutes or until toothpick inserted into center comes out clean.

Cool cake in pan on wire rack. DO NOT REMOVE CAKE FROM PAN. Frost cake with the following frosting recipe.

## *Frosting*

- 4 Tbsp. (½ stick) butter or margarine, softened
- ½ cup firmly packed brown sugar
- 3 Tbsp. cream or milk
- 1 cup *less 1 Tbsp.* wheat flakes or corn flakes, crushed into crumbs

Preheat broiler to high.

Combine all *Frosting* ingredients in a bowl. Spread *Frosting* on top of cake.

Place frosted cake under broiler. Close door and **watch cake every second**. Ready when top bubbles.

Cool cake in pan on wire rack for 5 minutes before serving.

Makes 12 servings.

*Continued ...*

# Desserts

*Every so often everyone has a lazy day at home. Back in the early 1960's Anne Wolf enhanced her lazy days of fun with her children by baking this recipe given to her by an active seventy-year-old lady in her church group.*

*Anne's son Mark still remembers those days. He didn't have a computer or other sophisticated gadgets to amuse him for hours. Instead he had lazy days of playing outside, reading, or just using his imagination. For some reason he imagined that he was very poor. To this day whenever he wants his mother to bake his favorite cake he'll say: "Can you make the cake you made when we were really poor?"*

*Although the recipe is simple to make, it's by no means quick. Even the Quick oats must stand for 20 minutes. This is one recipe geared to slacken your pace.*

# NANA'S SCOTTISH SHORTBREAD

    1 cup sugar
    1 cup (2 sticks) butter (softened)
    1 cup Crisco (softened)
    1 egg
    4 cups all-purpose flour, sifted,
        plus extra if needed

Preheat oven to 325 degrees.

Cream sugar, butter, Crisco, and egg by hand.

Work in sifted flour, one cup at a time, to cream mixture. Dough is ready when it comes easily away from the bowl.

Form 3 balls of dough. Roll each ball on a floured board, one at a time, to form a ½-inch-thick circle. Cut according to diagram below. Place ½ inch apart on **ungreased** baking sheet.

Bake at 325 degrees for approximately 20 minutes, or until cookies are *almost* golden brown.

Makes 4 dozen cookies.

**Note:** The original recipe uses lard instead of Crisco.

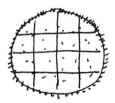

*Continued ...*

# Desserts

" *This is a tricky recipe. The ingredients were not measured by my Nana. She would feel the dough to see if it was ready to roll out. When it was time to bake she would guess at the oven temperature. She judged by the color when the cookies were done."*

*Margaret Carroll continues her Nana's tradition of making Scottish Shortbread every Christmas. This was Nana's special Christmas present to family and friends. In order to have enough cookies to fill a tin Nana would start baking her shortbread cookies a couple of weeks before Christmas. Everyone always looked forward to Nana's Scottish Shortbread. Because of this Nana kept her recipe a secret.*

*Over the years Margaret's mother somehow acquired her mother's recipe and passed it on to her daughter. Today Margaret strictly follows the recipe, using lard. Not wanting to use animal products, I substituted Crisco for the lard, then had Margaret sample them.*

*"How do they compare with your cookies?" I asked.*

*"The same texture and looks. They're delicious. There's really no difference except that mine are a little saltier," Margaret replied. "Maybe I'll use Crisco in the future and just add a pinch of salt."*

*I found the ones I make with Crisco to be rich and crumbly. Perfect. They melt in your mouth!*

# HERMIT COOKIES

1 cup sugar
½ cup shortening
½ cup molasses
½ cup lukewarm coffee
1 tsp. baking soda, dissolved in the coffee
3 cups all-purpose flour
1 tsp. ground cloves
1 tsp. ground cinnamon
½ tsp. salt
1 egg, beaten
1 cup raisins
1 cup chopped walnuts

Preheat oven to 350 degrees.

Grease cookie sheets.

In a large bowl, with mixer at low speed, cream sugar and shortening. Stir in molasses. Add coffee with dissolved baking soda. Mix at low speed until combined.

Sift together: flour, cloves, cinnamon, salt. Add to creamed mixture, a little at a time, beating after each addition. Add beaten egg. Mix at medium speed until well blended.

Fold in raisins and walnuts.

Using a spatula evenly spread dough lengthwise to form long strips, not more than 1 inch wide.

*Continued ...*

 **Desserts**

*HERMIT COOKIES...Continued*

Flatten the dough with greased and floured hands.

Bake at 350 degrees for 10 minutes.

When cool, cut into pieces.

Makes approximately 4 dozen cookies.

" *This* is my all-time favorite cookie," Maureen Briggs said while munching on one of the Hermit Cookies I had baked that morning. "When I was growing up my mom, Jeanne McCarthy, made these cookies often, and still does. She inherited this recipe from her mom."

Maureen added: "It's the coffee in these cookies that makes them special. This recipe goes back over 50 years. It can never be outdated."

That same day I shared the Hermits with people at work. Their reactions were: "Do you have any more?" "I haven't had a hermit cookie like this in years!" "My mother used to make these when I was a kid."

If it's been a long time since you've revisited a childhood experience, or if you simply want to try something new, bake Hermit Cookies for yourself, your family, and friends. They're fun to make, and best of all, great to eat.

## PORTUGUESE BISCOITOS

8 cups King Arthur all-purpose flour
4 cups sugar
2½ Tbsp. baking powder
1 tsp. salt
1 cup (2 sticks) chilled butter, cut into small
 pieces
3 Tbsp. Crisco
7 eggs, plus extra if needed
1 beaten egg (to brush tops of biscoitos
 before baking)

Preheat oven to 325 degrees.

Place flour, sugar, baking powder, and salt in a large
bowl. Mix well.

*Continued ...*

 **Desserts**

Using a pastry cutter cut in butter and Crisco until mixture forms crumbs.

Add eggs, two at a time. Blend well by hand, gathering dough into a ball. If dough sticks to hand, add an extra egg.

Shape small amounts of dough into ropes: Take a tablespoon of dough; roll dough between palms of hands to form a six-inch rope. Press ends together to form a circle. Place biscoitos on cookie sheet lined with foil. Brush tops with beaten egg.

Bake at 325 degrees for approximately 25 minutes, or until cookies are golden brown. Cool completely **before** removing biscoitos from foil. (If cookie sheet is needed for next batch, remove foil with biscoitos and set aside for cooling.)

Makes 8 dozen biscoitos.

*L*inda Eaton received a large tin of these traditional Portuguese cookies from "a little old Portuguese lady." This was her way of thanking Linda for being so kind to her in a time of need. After tasting them and sharing them with family and friends, Linda knew she had to have the recipe

She called the lady and asked her if she would share the recipe with her. First, the lady wanted to make more biscoitos to give Linda. "No, I can't have you do that. I want to make them myself."

Without hesitation the lady gave her this recipe, half in English and half in Portuguese. Linda still has the three little cube-size papers from twenty-five years ago. She vividly remembers some of the lady's instructions: "a coffee mug of sugar; mix by hand; add an extra egg if dough sticks to fingers."

For those who don't read Portuguese Linda wrote the entire recipe in English. She also translated vague measurements, such as "a coffee mug of sugar," to exact amounts.

The little old Portuguese lady? We don't know where she is. Probably gone, but Linda's memories of her still live on.

# MA'S CHRISTMAS COOKIES

 **Desserts**

# THUMB PRINT COOKIES

1 cup all-purpose flour, sifted **twice**
½ cup (1 stick) butter, softened
¼ cup brown sugar
1 egg yolk
½ tsp. vanilla extract
1 egg white, beaten with a fork
• chopped walnuts
  (to cover cookies before baking)
• various fruit jams

Preheat oven to 350 degrees.

Grease cookie sheets.

Cream butter and sugar with a spoon. Stir in egg yolk and vanilla.

Using a fork at first, mix in **twice**-sifted flour. Then blend well by hand until dough forms a ball.

Shape small amounts of dough into one-inch balls. Roll each ball in egg white, then in chopped walnuts. Place one inch apart on greased cookie sheet.

Bake at 350 degrees for **4 minutes.**

Remove from oven. Press your thumb in the center of each cookie to form a hole. Fill the hole with jam. (Do not overfill.)

Return to oven. Bake for 8 minutes.

Makes 2 dozen cookies.

# CHOCOLATE BON-BON COOKIES

½ cup (1 stick) butter, softened
¼ cup confectioners' sugar
1 tsp. vanilla extract
1 cup all-purpose flour, sifted
⅛ tsp. salt
1 oz. chocolate, melted
• chocolate icing (to dip cookies after baking)

Preheat oven to 350 degrees.

Cream butter, sugar, and vanilla. Thoroughly blend in sifted flour and salt with a spoon. Stir in melted chocolate until well blended.

Shape small amounts of dough into one-inch balls. Place one inch apart on **ungreased** cookie sheets.

Bake at 350 degrees for 10 to 12 minutes.

Cool slightly.

Top with chocolate icing. Put cookies on wire rack to dry.

Makes 2 dozen cookies.

*Continued ...*

*CHOCOLATE BON-BON COOKIES . . . Continued*

## Richard's Suggestions

❖ Fill center of cookies with chopped nuts, maraschino cherries (cut in half and patted dry), or chopped dates.

❖ Chocolate icing: Melt 1 oz. unsweetened chocolate and 1 Tbsp. butter in the microwave. Add ½ cup confectioners' sugar and 1 Tbsp. milk. Stir until well blended.

# CHRISTMAS CHEWS

¾ cup all-purpose flour, sifted
1 tsp. baking powder
¼ tsp. salt
1 cup dates, chopped
¾ cup pecans, chopped
¾ cup shredded coconut
2 eggs, well-beaten with a fork
½ tsp. grated orange zest

Preheat oven to 350 degrees.

Line a square pan, 8- x 8- x 2-inches, with wax paper. Grease the wax paper.

Combine sifted flour, baking powder, and salt. Add dates, pecans, and coconut. Stir with a spoon. Add well-beaten eggs and orange zest. Stir until thoroughly combined.

Spread dough in already lined and greased pan.

Bake at 350 degrees for 10 to 15 minutes or until set. **Do not over cook** (will get too hard).

Let stand on wire rack for 5 minutes.

Remove from pan. Cool.

Cut into bars, about 2 x 1½ inches.

Makes 2 dozen cookies.

*Continued ...*

*Every year friends and family of Richard Marrocco enjoy attending his Christmas open house, not just for the decorations, but also for the food he prepares. Richard loves Christmas so much that he decorates all his rooms for the season. He starts weeks ahead, packing away his year-round items to create space for displaying his special collections.*

*Among the many gourmet items Richard bakes for this festive occasion he always includes a tray of Ma's Christmas Cookies. Richard's mother, Lena, shared his love for Christmas. Every year she would bake these cookies at Christmas time. Richard continues her tradition, always remembering the joy she had for Christmas and how she instilled the same in him.*

*Being a guest at Richard's house is always a special treat—not just at Christmas, but year 'round.*